Date: _____

Teacher Message:

Stud[ent]

Dear teacher,

MW01076812

Practice Time	MON.	TUE.	WED.	THUR.	FRI.	SAT.	SUN.	TOTAL

Technique Book, Scales, etc.

_____

_____

_____

Lesson Book

_____

_____

_____

_____

Performance Book

_____

_____

Other Books and Solos

_____

_____

_____

Theory Book

pages _____, _____, _____, _____

Practice Suggestions:

_____

_____

_____

_____

_____

_____

_____

_____

_____

_____

theory notes:

Date: _____

Teacher Message:

Student | Parent Postcard

Dear teacher,

Practice Time	MON.	TUE.	WED.	THUR.	FRI.	SAT.	SUN.	TOTAL

Technique Book, Scales, etc.

_____
_____
_____

Practice Suggestions:

_____
_____
_____

Lesson Book

_____
_____
_____
_____
_____

_____
_____
_____
_____

Performance Book

_____
_____
_____

_____
_____

Other Books and Solos

_____
_____
_____

_____
_____

theory notes:

Theory Book

pages ____, ____, ____, ____

Date: _____

Teacher Message:

Student / Parent Postcard

Dear teacher,

Practice Time	MON.	TUE.	WED.	THUR.	FRI.	SAT.	SUN.	TOTAL

Technique Book, Scales, etc.

_____
_____
_____

Practice Suggestions:

_____
_____
_____

Lesson Book

_____
_____
_____
_____
_____

_____
_____
_____
_____
_____

Performance Book

_____
_____
_____

_____
_____
_____

Other Books and Solos

_____
_____
_____

_____
_____

theory notes:

Theory Book

pages ____, ____, ____, ____

_____
_____
_____
_____

_____
_____
_____
_____

Date: _____

Teacher Message:

Student / Parent Postcard

Dear teacher,

Practice Time	MON.	TUE.	WED.	THUR.	FRI.	SAT.	SUN.	TOTAL

Technique Book, Scales, etc.

_____
_____
_____

Lesson Book

_____
_____
_____
_____
_____

Performance Book

_____
_____
_____

Other Books and Solos

_____
_____
_____

Theory Book

pages _____, _____, _____, _____

Practice Suggestions:

_____
_____
_____
_____
_____
_____
_____
_____
_____
_____
_____

theory notes:

_____
_____
_____
_____
_____
_____
_____
_____
_____

Date: _____

Teacher Message:

Student / Parent Postcard

Dear teacher,

Practice Time	MON.	TUE.	WED.	THUR.	FRI.	SAT.	SUN.	TOTAL

Technique Book, Scales, etc.

_____
_____
_____

Practice Suggestions:

_____
_____
_____

Lesson Book

_____
_____
_____
_____
_____

_____
_____
_____
_____
_____
_____

Performance Book

_____
_____
_____

_____
_____
_____

Other Books and Solos

_____
_____
_____

_____
_____

theory notes:

Theory Book

pages ____, ____, ____, ____

Date: _____

Teacher Message:

Student / Parent Postcard

Dear teacher,

Practice Time	MON.	TUE.	WED.	THUR.	FRI.	SAT.	SUN.	TOTAL

Technique Book, Scales, etc.

_____
_____
_____

Lesson Book

_____
_____
_____
_____
_____

Performance Book

_____
_____
_____

Other Books and Solos

_____
_____
_____

Theory Book

pages _____, _____, _____, _____

Practice Suggestions:

_____
_____
_____
_____

_____
_____
_____
_____
_____

_____
_____
_____

_____
_____

theory notes:

_____
_____
_____
_____
_____

_____
_____

Date: _____

Teacher Message:

Student / Parent Postcard

Dear teacher,

Practice Time	MON.	TUE.	WED.	THUR.	FRI.	SAT.	SUN.	TOTAL

Technique Book, Scales, etc.

_____
_____
_____

Practice Suggestions:

_____
_____
_____
_____

Lesson Book

_____
_____
_____
_____
_____

_____
_____
_____
_____
_____

Performance Book

_____
_____
_____

_____
_____
_____

Other Books and Solos

_____
_____
_____

_____
_____
_____

theory notes:

Theory Book

pages _____, _____, _____, _____

_____
_____
_____
_____

_____
_____
_____

Date: _____

Teacher Message:

Student / Parent Postcard

Dear teacher,

Practice Time	MON.	TUE.	WED.	THUR.	FRI.	SAT.	SUN.	TOTAL

Technique Book, Scales, etc.

_____
_____
_____

Practice Suggestions:

_____
_____
_____

Lesson Book

_____
_____
_____
_____
_____

_____
_____
_____

Performance Book

_____
_____
_____

_____
_____

Other Books and Solos

_____
_____
_____

_____

Theory Book

pages _____, _____, _____, _____

theory notes:

Date: _____

Teacher Message:

Student / Parent Postcard

Dear teacher,

Practice Time	MON.	TUE.	WED.	THUR.	FRI.	SAT.	SUN.	TOTAL

Technique Book, Scales, etc.

_____
_____
_____

Practice Suggestions:

_____
_____
_____

Lesson Book

_____
_____
_____
_____
_____

_____
_____
_____
_____
_____

Performance Book

_____
_____
_____

_____
_____
_____

Other Books and Solos

_____
_____
_____

_____
_____

Theory Book

pages ____, ____, ____, ____

theory notes:

Date: _____

Teacher Message:

Student / Parent Postcard

Dear teacher,

Practice Time	MON.	TUE.	WED.	THUR.	FRI.	SAT.	SUN.	TOTAL

Technique Book, Scales, etc.

_____
_____
_____

Lesson Book

_____
_____
_____
_____
_____

Performance Book

_____
_____

Other Books and Solos

_____
_____
_____

Theory Book

pages _____, _____, _____, _____

Practice Suggestions:

_____
_____
_____
_____
_____
_____
_____
_____
_____
_____
_____

theory notes:

_____
_____
_____
_____
_____
_____

Date: _____

Teacher Message:

Student / Parent Postcard

Dear teacher,

Practice Time	MON.	TUE.	WED.	THUR.	FRI.	SAT.	SUN.	TOTAL

Technique Book, Scales, etc.

_____
_____
_____

Lesson Book

_____
_____
_____
_____

Performance Book

_____
_____

Other Books and Solos

_____
_____
_____

Theory Book

pages _____, _____, _____, _____

Practice Suggestions:

_____
_____
_____

_____
_____
_____
_____

_____
_____

_____
_____

theory notes:

_____
_____
_____
_____

_____
_____
_____

Date: _____

Teacher Message:

Student / Parent Postcard

Dear teacher,

Practice Time	MON.	TUE.	WED.	THUR.	FRI.	SAT.	SUN.	TOTAL

Technique Book, Scales, etc.

_____
_____
_____

Practice Suggestions:

_____
_____
_____

Lesson Book

_____
_____
_____
_____
_____

_____
_____
_____
_____

Performance Book

_____
_____
_____

_____
_____

Other Books and Solos

_____
_____

_____

Theory Book

pages _____, _____, _____, _____

theory notes:

_____
_____
_____
_____
_____

_____
_____
_____

Date: _____

Teacher Message:

Student / Parent Postcard

Dear teacher,

Practice Time	MON.	TUE.	WED.	THUR.	FRI.	SAT.	SUN.	TOTAL

Technique Book, Scales, etc.

_____

_____

_____

Practice Suggestions:

_____

_____

_____

Lesson Book

_____

_____

_____

_____

_____

_____

_____

_____

Performance Book

_____

_____

_____

_____

_____

Other Books and Solos

_____

_____

_____

_____

theory notes:

Theory Book

pages _____, _____, _____, _____

Date: _____

Teacher Message:

Student / Parent Postcard

Dear teacher,

Practice Time	MON.	TUE.	WED.	THUR.	FRI.	SAT.	SUN.	TOTAL

Technique Book, Scales, etc.

_____
_____
_____

Practice Suggestions:

_____
_____
_____

Lesson Book

_____
_____
_____
_____
_____

_____
_____
_____
_____
_____

Performance Book

_____
_____

_____
_____

Other Books and Solos

_____
_____
_____

_____

theory notes:

Theory Book

pages _____, _____, _____, _____

_____
_____
_____
_____
_____
_____

Date: _____

Teacher Message:

Student / Parent Postcard

Dear teacher,

Practice Time	MON.	TUE.	WED.	THUR.	FRI.	SAT.	SUN.	TOTAL

Technique Book, Scales, etc.

_____
_____
_____

Lesson Book

_____
_____
_____
_____
_____

Performance Book

_____
_____
_____

Other Books and Solos

_____
_____
_____

Theory Book

pages _____, _____, _____, _____

Practice Suggestions:

_____
_____
_____

_____
_____
_____
_____
_____

_____
_____
_____

_____
_____

theory notes:

Date: _____

Teacher Message:

Student / Parent Postcard

Dear teacher,

Practice Time	MON.	TUE.	WED.	THUR.	FRI.	SAT.	SUN.	TOTAL

Technique Book, Scales, etc.

_____
_____
_____

Practice Suggestions:

_____
_____
_____

Lesson Book

_____
_____
_____
_____
_____

_____
_____
_____
_____

Performance Book

_____
_____
_____

_____
_____

Other Books and Solos

_____
_____
_____

_____
_____

theory notes:

Theory Book

pages ____, ____, ____, ____

Date: _____

Teacher Message:

Student / Parent Postcard

Dear teacher,

Practice Time	MON.	TUE.	WED.	THUR.	FRI.	SAT.	SUN.	TOTAL

Technique Book, Scales, etc.

_____

_____

_____

Practice Suggestions:

_____

_____

_____

Lesson Book

_____

_____

_____

_____

_____

Performance Book

_____

_____

_____

Other Books and Solos

_____

_____

_____

theory notes:

Theory Book

pages ____, ____, ____, ____

Date: _____

Teacher Message:

Student / Parent Postcard

Dear teacher,

Practice Time	MON.	TUE.	WED.	THUR.	FRI.	SAT.	SUN.	TOTAL

Technique Book, Scales, etc.

_____
_____
_____

Lesson Book

_____
_____
_____
_____
_____

Performance Book

_____
_____
_____

Other Books and Solos

_____
_____
_____

Theory Book

pages _____, _____, _____, _____

Practice Suggestions:

_____
_____
_____
_____
_____
_____
_____
_____
_____

theory notes:

Date: _____

Teacher Message:

Student / Parent Postcard

Dear teacher,

Practice Time	MON.	TUE.	WED.	THUR.	FRI.	SAT.	SUN.	TOTAL

Technique Book, Scales, etc.

_____
_____
_____

Lesson Book

_____
_____
_____
_____
_____

Performance Book

_____
_____
_____

Other Books and Solos

_____
_____
_____

Theory Book

pages _____, _____, _____, _____

Practice Suggestions:

_____
_____
_____

_____
_____
_____
_____
_____

_____
_____
_____

theory notes:

Date: _____

Teacher Message:

Student / Parent Postcard

Dear teacher,

Practice Time	MON.	TUE.	WED.	THUR.	FRI.	SAT.	SUN.	TOTAL

Technique Book, Scales, etc.

_____
_____
_____

Lesson Book

_____
_____
_____
_____
_____

Performance Book

_____
_____
_____

Other Books and Solos

_____
_____
_____

Theory Book

pages _____, _____, _____, _____

Practice Suggestions:

_____
_____
_____
_____
_____
_____
_____
_____
_____
_____
_____
_____

theory notes:

Date: _____

Teacher Message:

Student / Parent Postcard

Dear teacher,

Practice Time	MON.	TUE.	WED.	THUR.	FRI.	SAT.	SUN.	TOTAL

Technique Book, Scales, etc.

_____
_____
_____

Lesson Book

_____
_____
_____
_____
_____

Performance Book

_____
_____
_____

Other Books and Solos

_____
_____
_____

Theory Book

pages _____, _____, _____, _____

Practice Suggestions:

_____
_____
_____

_____
_____
_____
_____
_____

_____
_____
_____

theory notes:

Date: _____

Teacher Message:

Student / Parent Postcard

Dear teacher,

Practice Time	MON.	TUE.	WED.	THUR.	FRI.	SAT.	SUN.	TOTAL

Technique Book, Scales, etc.

_____
_____
_____

Practice Suggestions:

_____
_____
_____

Lesson Book

_____
_____
_____
_____
_____

_____
_____
_____
_____
_____

Performance Book

_____
_____
_____

_____
_____
_____

Other Books and Solos

_____
_____
_____

_____
_____

Theory Book

pages _____, _____, _____, _____

theory notes:

_____
_____
_____
_____
_____

_____
_____
_____
_____

Date: _____

Teacher Message:

Student / Parent Postcard

Dear teacher,

Practice Time	MON.	TUE.	WED.	THUR.	FRI.	SAT.	SUN.	TOTAL

Technique Book, Scales, etc.

_____
_____
_____

Practice Suggestions:

_____
_____
_____

Lesson Book

_____
_____
_____
_____
_____

_____
_____
_____
_____
_____

Performance Book

_____
_____
_____

_____
_____

Other Books and Solos

_____
_____
_____

_____
_____

Theory Book

pages _____, _____, _____, _____

theory notes:

Date: _____

Teacher Message:

Student / Parent Postcard

Dear teacher,

Practice Time	MON.	TUE.	WED.	THUR.	FRI.	SAT.	SUN.	TOTAL

Technique Book, Scales, etc.

_____
_____
_____

Practice Suggestions:

_____
_____
_____

Lesson Book

_____
_____
_____
_____
_____

_____
_____
_____
_____
_____

Performance Book

_____
_____
_____

_____
_____

Other Books and Solos

_____
_____
_____

_____
_____

Theory Book

pages _____, _____, _____, _____

theory notes:

_____
_____
_____
_____
_____
_____

_____
_____
_____
_____
_____

Date: _____

Teacher Message:

Student / Parent Postcard

Dear teacher,

Practice Time	MON.	TUE.	WED.	THUR.	FRI.	SAT.	SUN.	TOTAL

Technique Book, Scales, etc.

_____
_____
_____

Practice Suggestions:

_____
_____
_____

Lesson Book

_____
_____
_____
_____

_____
_____
_____

Performance Book

_____
_____
_____

_____
_____

Other Books and Solos

_____
_____
_____

theory notes:

Theory Book

pages _____, _____, _____, _____

Date: _____

Teacher Message:

Student / Parent Postcard

Dear teacher,

Practice Time	MON.	TUE.	WED.	THUR.	FRI.	SAT.	SUN.	TOTAL

Technique Book, Scales, etc.

_____
_____
_____

Practice Suggestions:

_____
_____
_____

Lesson Book

_____
_____
_____
_____
_____

_____
_____
_____
_____

Performance Book

_____
_____
_____

_____
_____
_____

Other Books and Solos

_____
_____
_____

_____

theory notes:

Theory Book

pages _____, _____, _____, _____

Date: _____

Teacher Message:

Student / Parent Postcard

Dear teacher,

Practice Time	MON.	TUE.	WED.	THUR.	FRI.	SAT.	SUN.	TOTAL

Technique Book, Scales, etc.

_____

_____

_____

Practice Suggestions:

_____

_____

_____

Lesson Book

_____

_____

_____

_____

_____

_____

Performance Book

_____

_____

_____

Other Books and Solos

_____

_____

_____

Theory Book

pages ____, ____, ____, ____

theory notes:

_____
_____
_____
_____
_____

_____
_____
_____

Date: _____

Teacher Message:

Student / Parent Postcard

Dear teacher,

Practice Time	MON.	TUE.	WED.	THUR.	FRI.	SAT.	SUN.	TOTAL

Technique Book, Scales, etc.

_____

_____

_____

Practice Suggestions:

_____

_____

_____

Lesson Book

_____

_____

_____

_____

_____

_____

_____

_____

_____

Performance Book

_____

_____

_____

_____

_____

Other Books and Solos

_____

_____

_____

_____

Theory Book

pages _____, _____, _____, _____

theory notes:

_____

_____

_____

_____

_____

_____

_____

_____

Date: _____

Teacher Message:

Student / Parent Postcard

Dear teacher,

Practice Time	MON.	TUE.	WED.	THUR.	FRI.	SAT.	SUN.	TOTAL

Technique Book, Scales, etc.

_____
_____
_____

Lesson Book

_____
_____
_____
_____

Performance Book

_____
_____
_____

Other Books and Solos

_____
_____
_____

Practice Suggestions:

_____
_____
_____
_____
_____
_____
_____
_____
_____
_____

theory notes:

Theory Book

pages _____, _____, _____, _____

Date: _____

Teacher Message:

Student / Parent Postcard

Dear teacher,

Practice Time	MON.	TUE.	WED.	THUR.	FRI.	SAT.	SUN.	TOTAL

Technique Book, Scales, etc.

_____
_____
_____

Practice Suggestions:

_____
_____
_____
_____

Lesson Book

_____
_____
_____
_____
_____

_____
_____
_____
_____

Performance Book

_____
_____

_____
_____

Other Books and Solos

_____
_____
_____

_____

theory notes:

Theory Book

pages _____, _____, _____, _____

Date: _____

Teacher Message:

Student / Parent Postcard

Dear teacher,

Practice Time	MON.	TUE.	WED.	THUR.	FRI.	SAT.	SUN.	TOTAL

Technique Book, Scales, etc.

_____
_____
_____

Practice Suggestions:

_____
_____
_____

Lesson Book

_____
_____
_____
_____

_____
_____
_____
_____

Performance Book

_____
_____
_____

_____
_____

Other Books and Solos

_____
_____
_____

_____
_____

Theory Book

pages _____, _____, _____, _____

theory notes:

Date: _____

Teacher Message:

Student / Parent Postcard

Dear teacher,

Practice Time	MON.	TUE.	WED.	THUR.	FRI.	SAT.	SUN.	TOTAL

Technique Book, Scales, etc.

_____

_____

_____

Practice Suggestions:

_____

_____

Lesson Book

_____

_____

_____

_____

_____

_____

_____

_____

_____

Performance Book

_____

_____

_____

_____

_____

Other Books and Solos

_____

_____

_____

_____

theory notes:

Theory Book

pages _____, _____, _____, _____

Date: _____

Teacher Message:

Student / Parent Postcard

Dear teacher,

Practice Time	MON.	TUE.	WED.	THUR.	FRI.	SAT.	SUN.	TOTAL

Technique Book, Scales, etc.

_____
_____
_____

Practice Suggestions:

_____
_____
_____

Lesson Book

_____
_____
_____
_____
_____

_____
_____
_____
_____
_____

Performance Book

_____
_____
_____

_____
_____
_____

Other Books and Solos

_____
_____
_____

_____
_____

theory notes:

Theory Book

pages _____, _____, _____, _____

Date: _____

🍎 **Teacher Message:**

Student / Parent Postcard

Dear teacher,

Practice Time	MON.	TUE.	WED.	THUR.	FRI.	SAT.	SUN.	TOTAL

Technique Book, Scales, etc.

_____
_____
_____

Lesson Book

_____
_____
_____
_____
_____

Performance Book

_____
_____
_____

Other Books and Solos

_____
_____
_____

Theory Book

pages _____, _____, _____, _____

Practice Suggestions:

_____
_____
_____
_____
_____
_____
_____
_____
_____
_____
_____
_____
_____

theory notes:

_____
_____
_____
_____
_____
_____
_____
_____

Date: _____

Teacher Message:

Student / Parent Postcard

Dear teacher,

Practice Time	MON.	TUE.	WED.	THUR.	FRI.	SAT.	SUN.	TOTAL

Technique Book, Scales, etc.

_____

_____

_____

Practice Suggestions:

_____

_____

_____

Lesson Book

_____

_____

_____

_____

_____

_____

_____

_____

_____

Performance Book

_____

_____

_____

_____

_____

Other Books and Solos

_____

_____

_____

_____

_____

Theory Book

pages _____, _____, _____, _____

theory notes:

Date: _____

Teacher Message:

Student / Parent Postcard

Dear teacher,

Practice Time	MON.	TUE.	WED.	THUR.	FRI.	SAT.	SUN.	TOTAL

Technique Book, Scales, etc.

_____
_____
_____

Practice Suggestions:

_____
_____
_____

Lesson Book

_____
_____
_____
_____
_____

_____
_____
_____
_____

Performance Book

_____
_____
_____

_____
_____
_____

Other Books and Solos

_____
_____
_____

_____

theory notes:

Theory Book

pages ____, ____, ____, ____

_____
_____
_____
_____

_____
_____
_____

Date: _____

Teacher Message:

Student / Parent Postcard

Dear teacher,

Practice Time	MON.	TUE.	WED.	THUR.	FRI.	SAT.	SUN.	TOTAL

Technique Book, Scales, etc.

_____
_____
_____

Practice Suggestions:

_____
_____
_____

Lesson Book

_____
_____
_____
_____
_____

_____
_____
_____
_____
_____

Performance Book

_____
_____
_____

_____
_____
_____

Other Books and Solos

_____
_____
_____

_____
_____

Theory Book

pages _____, _____, _____, _____

theory notes:

Date: _____

Teacher Message:

Student / Parent Postcard

Dear teacher,

Practice Time	MON.	TUE.	WED.	THUR.	FRI.	SAT.	SUN.	TOTAL

Technique Book, Scales, etc.

_____

_____

_____

Practice Suggestions:

_____

_____

_____

Lesson Book

_____

_____

_____

_____

_____

_____

_____

_____

Performance Book

_____

_____

_____

_____

Other Books and Solos

_____

_____

_____

_____

theory notes:

Theory Book

pages _____, _____, _____, _____

Date: _____

Teacher Message:

Student / Parent Postcard

Dear teacher,

Practice Time	MON.	TUE.	WED.	THUR.	FRI.	SAT.	SUN.	TOTAL

Technique Book, Scales, etc.

_____

_____

_____

Practice Suggestions:

_____

_____

_____

Lesson Book

_____

_____

_____

_____

_____

_____

_____

_____

_____

Performance Book

_____

_____

_____

_____

_____

_____

Other Books and Solos

_____

_____

_____

_____

_____

theory notes:

Theory Book

pages ____, ____, ____, ____

Date: _____

Teacher Message:

Student / Parent Postcard

Dear teacher,

Practice Time	MON.	TUE.	WED.	THUR.	FRI.	SAT.	SUN.	TOTAL

Technique Book, Scales, etc.

_____
_____
_____

Practice Suggestions:

_____
_____
_____

Lesson Book

_____
_____
_____
_____
_____

_____
_____
_____
_____

Performance Book

_____
_____
_____

_____
_____

Other Books and Solos

_____
_____
_____

_____

theory notes:

Theory Book

pages _____, _____, _____, _____

Date: _____

Teacher Message:

Student / Parent Postcard

Dear teacher,

Practice Time	MON.	TUE.	WED.	THUR.	FRI.	SAT.	SUN.	TOTAL

Technique Book, Scales, etc.

_____
_____
_____

Practice Suggestions:

_____
_____
_____

Lesson Book

_____
_____
_____
_____

_____
_____
_____
_____
_____

Performance Book

_____
_____
_____

_____
_____

Other Books and Solos

_____
_____
_____

_____
_____

Theory Book

pages ____, ____, ____, ____

theory notes:

Date: _____

Teacher Message:

Student / **Parent Postcard**

Dear teacher,

Practice Time	MON.	TUE.	WED.	THUR.	FRI.	SAT.	SUN.	TOTAL

Technique Book, Scales, etc.

_____

_____

_____

Practice Suggestions:

_____

_____

_____

Lesson Book

_____

_____

_____

_____

_____

_____

_____

_____

Performance Book

_____

_____

_____

_____

_____

Other Books and Solos

_____

_____

_____

theory notes:

Theory Book

pages _____, _____, _____, _____

_____
_____
_____
_____
_____

_____
_____
_____

Date: _____

🍎 **Teacher Message:**

Student / Parent Postcard

Dear teacher, ✏️

Practice Time	MON.	TUE.	WED.	THUR.	FRI.	SAT.	SUN.	TOTAL

Technique Book, Scales, etc.

_____
_____
_____

Practice Suggestions:

_____
_____
_____

Lesson Book

_____
_____
_____
_____
_____

_____
_____
_____
_____
_____

Performance Book

_____
_____
_____

_____
_____

Other Books and Solos

_____
_____
_____

Theory Book

pages _____, _____, _____, _____

theory notes:

Date: _____

Teacher Message:

Student / Parent Postcard

Dear teacher,

Practice Time	MON.	TUE.	WED.	THUR.	FRI.	SAT.	SUN.	TOTAL

Technique Book, Scales, etc.

_____

_____

_____

Practice Suggestions:

_____

_____

_____

Lesson Book

_____

_____

_____

_____

_____

_____

_____

_____

_____

Performance Book

_____

_____

_____

_____

_____

_____

Other Books and Solos

_____

_____

_____

_____

_____

_____

theory notes:

Theory Book

pages _____, _____, _____, _____

_____

_____

_____

_____

_____

_____

_____

Date: _____

Teacher Message:

Student / Parent Postcard

Dear teacher,

Practice Time	MON.	TUE.	WED.	THUR.	FRI.	SAT.	SUN.	TOTAL

Technique Book, Scales, etc.

Practice Suggestions:

Lesson Book

Performance Book

Other Books and Solos

theory notes:

Theory Book

pages _____, _____, _____, _____

Date: _____

Teacher Message:

Student / Parent Postcard

Dear teacher,

Practice Time	MON.	TUE.	WED.	THUR.	FRI.	SAT.	SUN.	TOTAL

Technique Book, Scales, etc.

_____

_____

_____

Practice Suggestions:

_____

_____

_____

Lesson Book

_____

_____

_____

_____

_____

_____

_____

_____

Performance Book

_____

_____

_____

_____

_____

Other Books and Solos

_____

_____

_____

_____

theory notes:

Theory Book

pages _____, _____, _____, _____

Date: _____

Teacher Message:

Student / Parent Postcard

Dear teacher,

Practice Time	MON.	TUE.	WED.	THUR.	FRI.	SAT.	SUN.	TOTAL

Technique Book, Scales, etc.

_____
_____
_____

Practice Suggestions:

_____
_____
_____

Lesson Book

_____
_____
_____
_____
_____

_____
_____
_____
_____

Performance Book

_____
_____
_____

_____
_____
_____

Other Books and Solos

_____
_____
_____

_____
_____

theory notes:

Theory Book

pages _____, _____, _____, _____

Date: _____

Teacher Message:

Student / Parent Postcard

Dear teacher,

Practice Time	MON.	TUE.	WED.	THUR.	FRI.	SAT.	SUN.	TOTAL

Technique Book, Scales, etc.

_____

_____

_____

Practice Suggestions:

_____

_____

_____

_____

Lesson Book

_____

_____

_____

_____

_____

_____

_____

_____

_____

_____

Performance Book

_____

_____

_____

_____

_____

_____

Other Books and Solos

_____

_____

_____

_____

_____

theory notes:

Theory Book

pages _____, _____, _____, _____

_____
_____
_____
_____

_____
_____
_____
_____

Date: _____

Teacher Message:

Student / Parent Postcard

Dear teacher,

Practice Time	MON.	TUE.	WED.	THUR.	FRI.	SAT.	SUN.	TOTAL

Technique Book, Scales, etc.

_____
_____
_____

Practice Suggestions:

_____
_____
_____

Lesson Book

_____
_____
_____
_____
_____

_____
_____
_____
_____
_____

Performance Book

_____
_____
_____

_____
_____

Other Books and Solos

_____
_____
_____

_____

theory notes:

Theory Book

pages _____, _____, _____, _____

_____
_____
_____
_____

_____
_____
_____

Date: _____

Teacher Message:

Student / Parent Postcard

Dear teacher,

Practice Time	MON.	TUE.	WED.	THUR.	FRI.	SAT.	SUN.	TOTAL

Technique Book, Scales, etc.

_____
_____
_____

Practice Suggestions:

_____
_____
_____

Lesson Book

_____
_____
_____
_____
_____

_____
_____
_____
_____

Performance Book

_____
_____

_____
_____

Other Books and Solos

_____
_____
_____

theory notes:

Theory Book

pages _____, _____, _____, _____

Date: _____

Teacher Message:

Student / Parent Postcard

Dear teacher,

Practice Time	MON.	TUE.	WED.	THUR.	FRI.	SAT.	SUN.	TOTAL

Technique Book, Scales, etc.

_____
_____
_____

Practice Suggestions:

_____
_____
_____

Lesson Book

_____
_____
_____
_____
_____

_____
_____
_____
_____
_____

Performance Book

_____
_____
_____

_____
_____
_____

Other Books and Solos

_____
_____
_____

_____
_____

theory notes:

Theory Book

pages _____, _____, _____, _____

Dictionary of Musical Terms

DYNAMIC MARKS

pp	*p*	*mp*	*mf*	*f*	*ff*
pianissimo very soft	*piano* soft	*mezzo piano* moderately soft	*mezzo forte* moderately loud	*forte* loud	*fortissimo* very loud

TEMPO MARKS

Adagio	*Andante*	*Moderato*	*Allegretto*	*Allegro*	*Vivace*
slowly	"walking speed"	moderate tempo	rather fast	fast and lively	very fast

SIGN	TERM	DEFINITION
accel.	*accelerando*	Gradually play faster.
(accent sign)	**accent**	Play this note louder.
	alla breve	Cut time. Short for $\frac{2}{2}$ time signature. The half note gets the beat. (Two-half note beats per measure.)
	Alberti bass	A left-hand accompaniment which outlines the notes of a chord using the pattern: bottom-top-middle-top.
	arpeggio	Rolled chord. Play the notes of the chord one at a time, rapidly, from bottom to top.
	a tempo	Resume the earlier tempo (speed).
	cadenza	A showy, solo passage which is usually played with rhythmic freedom.
	cantabile	Singing.
	Coda	Ending section. (A short *coda* is called a *codetta.*)
(crescendo sign)	*crescendo (cresc.)*	Play gradually louder.
D.C. al Fine	**Da Capo al Fine**	Return to the beginning and play until *Fine* (end).
	damper pedal	The right-foot pedal. It lifts the dampers off the strings which allows the strings to continue to ring.
(decrescendo sign)	*decrescendo*	Play gradually softer. Same as *diminuendo.*
(diminuendo sign)	*diminuendo (dim.)*	Play gradually softer. Same as *decrescendo.*
	dolce	Sweetly.
(fermata sign)	*fermata*	Hold this note longer than usual.
	Fine	End here.
1. || 2.	**1st and 2nd endings**	Play the 1st ending and take the repeat. Then play the 2nd ending, skipping over the 1st ending.
(grace note sign)	**grace note**	A decorative note, written in small type with a slash through the stem. Grace notes are played quickly, before the main tone.
	imitation	The restatement of a musical idea in a different "voice" (different hand or instrumental part).
	interval	The distance between two pitches (2nd, 3rd, 4th, 5th, etc.)
	legato	Play smoothly, connected.
	lento	Slow; slower than *Adagio.*
	loco	Play where written. (Follows an octave sign.)

	meno mosso	Less motion.
	molto	Very. For example, *molto rit.* means to make a big *ritard*.
	motive	Short musical idea.
Op.	**opus**	Work. A composer's compositions are often arranged in sequence, with each work given an *opus* number. Several pieces may be included in a single opus. (Op. 3, No. 1; Op. 3, No. 2; etc.)
8va – – ⌐	*ottava*	Play one octave higher than written. When 8va is below the staff, play one octave lower.
	pedal mark	Depress the damper pedal after the note or chord.
	pedal change	Lift the damper pedal as the note is played. Depress the pedal immediately after.
	phrase	A musical idea. Think of a phrase as a "musical sentence." It is shown in the music with a slur, also called a phrase mark.
	più mosso	More motion.
	poco	A little.
15ma	*quindicesima*	Play two octaves higher than written.
rit.	*ritardando*	Gradually slowing down.
	rubato	An expressive "give and take" of the tempo.
	sempre	Always. For example, *sempre staccato* means to continue playing staccato.
	sequence	A short musical pattern that is repeated on another pitch.
sfz or *sf*	*sforzando*	A sudden strong accent.
	simile	Similarly. Continue in the same way (same pedaling, same use of staccato, etc.).
	$\frac{6}{8}$ **time signature**	Six eighth-note beats per measure. Usually felt "in two" with the ♩. receiving the beat.
	slur	Connect the notes within a slur.
	sonata	An instrumental piece, usually with 3 movements.
	sonatina	A little sonata.
	staccato	Play *staccato* notes detached, disconnected.
	stress mark	Accent this note slightly.
	subito	Suddenly. For example, *subito piano* means suddenly soft.
	tempo	The speed of the music.
ten.	**tenuto**	Hold the note its full value.
	theme and variations	A musical form which states a musical idea (theme) followed by modified presentations of the theme (variations). The variations may change the rhythm, harmony, or time signature, etc.
	$\frac{3}{8}$ **time signature**	Three eighth-note beats per measure.
tr	**trill**	A quick repetition of the principal note with the note above it.
	triplet	Three eighth notes to a quarter-note beat.
	unison	Both hands playing the same note names and rhythm.
	vivace	Quickly, very lively.

My Favorite Pieces

(repertoire list)

title	composer	✔ if memorized
_____	_____	☐
_____	_____	☐
_____	_____	☐
_____	_____	☐
_____	_____	☐
_____	_____	☐
_____	_____	☐
_____	_____	☐
_____	_____	☐
_____	_____	☐
_____	_____	☐
_____	_____	☐
_____	_____	☐
_____	_____	☐
_____	_____	☐
_____	_____	☐
_____	_____	☐
_____	_____	☐
_____	_____	☐

FF116